Emotional Alchemist

Poems

Written by: Alina Ramirez

This book is dedicated to :

Karina Ramirez, Sierra Gambala,
Khloie Partido, and Emilie Simpson

Thank you for creating a *Safe Space* for
me to continue to grow, heal, and create.

Identity Crisis

She took one look in the mirror,
and no longer recognizes who is staring back at her.
Where has she gone?

I go to place my hand on the mirror.
"You are beautiful", I tell her.

She welcomes me with tears dripping with sorrow,
a face full of burning mistrust, followed by a head
being weighed down by all her thoughts.

I can no longer see her, for she is a blur.
I am trying my best to sift through the misery,
But I am afraid that was the last time I'll ever see her,
for she has gone with the others, and on to the next.

I wipe her tears and welcome the new face reflecting.

Ugly Metamorphosis

It does not take much to give bad thoughts wings.
Mine fly every night, though never to be discovered.

The wind carries and allows them to dance in unison,
Sing in perfect harmony.
Speak confidently.

The owls turn their heads and call out for more.
The sirens blare closer, somehow making the swaying
of the leaves sound like ocean waves.

Lingering along the stars and filtering through the
constellations, I can see them making their way in
perfect route, with no intention of stopping and
with plans on arriving on time.

The closer they get, the weaker I grow.

Twisted

Pinned me up against the wall,
blindfolded me.
Tied my arms above my head and wrapped yourself
around me,
Begging me to let you in, all while I was drowning.

You begged for control, forgetting that you had it all
along.
My no frustrated you, had you on your knees,
kissing the tile on the floor.

I take the rope and tie you this time,
And suffocate you with my words.
But your disgust did not discriminate and lingered
all night,
Inebriated by the twisted fantasies within your mind.

Tangible

The only permanent thing in life is change.
It occurs whenever it feels like it is time,
whether we like it or not.

Yet somehow, you've managed to permanently alter
my DNA simply with your words.

We laughed, we cried, we danced, we kissed.
We hugged and even slept on the sand.

All those memories stayed,
but unfortunately you could not.
It's okay, I'm okay, I say with a smile on my face,

Holding back the tears I shed every February.

Sworn to Secrecy

Took my hand in yours as we watched the stars.

You tell me how much you crave privacy,
So we play a game of hide and seek.

Direct me to hide during the waking hours.
And promise to seek me in the evening.

I've grown bored watching the paint peel off my
walls. The sunlight peeking through my window
burns me, and I am finding myself glued to the hands
on the clock,

Believing if I hold on tight enough to them, they will
somehow be fueled by my waking desire to be in your
arms. But the clock strikes, and you are nowhere to
be found. So I continue to hide,

Hoping to be seeked.

Homebody in Traffic

I hate being stuck in traffic.

But I hope we catch it every time I am with you.

Because I do not want to go home.

I want the day to last forever.

I want to catch every red light and stop sign.

I want road closures and detours.

I want to become stranded hours away from home.

I want to laugh and pass the time as we wait for help.

I want your arms around me as the night breeze sets in.

Because you are home in human form.

And home is where I want to be.

I am, a homebody.

Lingering Twit

It’s so dark underground.

And yet somehow, you are still the shadow that lurks behind me.
I guess I took a wrong turn somewhere.

It's so dark underground.

I hold onto the anger so tight that it burns a hole in my heart.
I'm shouting, screaming.
Is it not enough? Am I not enough?
What is it? Acerbic wit?
It’s nothing if not personal, I suppose.
So I continue to follow - I just hope you get lost.
How could you not?

It's so dark underground.

Photographic Memory

The camera shutters desperately before it loses the
golden hour hues.
Capturing the foul memories that were picked out
from the tallest apple tree.
During their season as well.
The flavor is striking.
Unforgettable.

Developed them right away and showcased them all
to the entire town.
Everyone praised you for your ability to capture their
curiosity and millions of questions that encapsulated
their entire being.

The evening is burned into me like the cigarettes you
put out with your forearm.
Then tucked away in the scars that have faded with
time.

Suddenly everyone's memory is of an elephant's

Sometimes even my own mind.

Ready? 1... 2...3

Smile!

Beauty is Scaled

I look down at the number.
A teardrop falls, magnifying it.
Mocking me.
Wanting me to see it and consume it.

I grab every part of me I hate and scold it like a child that made a mess.

I grab a marker and circle everything I want to be different.
I soon find my entire body covered in red marker.
Smearing all over due to my tears falling on my body.
Until I am covered entirely in red ink.

I'd rather be anyone but me right now.

Time

The love I have for you is cynical.

Tied together with a pretty red ribbon.

Kissed with the idea of it ever being something worth fighting for.

All while being drenched with my lust.

Avoidance

I don't think I was supposed to hear that.
I read in between the lines and try to form a narrative
that will continue to make me see the good within
you.

I don't want this to die out.
So I run as far away from the reality of it all as fast as
I can.
Before it catches me and tells me it's time to go.

Because I am not ready yet.
I want to stay just a little bit longer.
It's nice here, quite cozy.

Your lies are a warm blanket,
and your manipulation is a hot cup of tea.
Your body is the perfect place to rest after a long day.

You ask me if I'm ready to go,
but all I hear is to stay a little longer, so I do.
But, my bags are packed and waiting for me at the
door.

I am not ready. I think I'll stay for tea once more.
Would you ever so kindly hand me that blanket?

The Road Most Traveled

You are an expert at pretending to be authentic.
Too much of an expert at spoon feeding my ego.

All while your hand finds a place to rest on my thigh
While the other steers us to a place with no
destination.

Until the amnesia appears.
And you suddenly forget who you are with.
Suddenly lose your desire and the loose thread
unravels the sewn heart.
And say it's time for you to go.

Sweet Pea

I do not know you.
But every bit of the idea of you has found a place to call
home within the walls of my heart.
You sing and dance all night there.

Then it suddenly goes silent,
and I wonder if you've grown tired.
Again, I don't even know you,
but felt the need to let you in.
Confessed with my tongue many things
the waking world could never fathom.

You ignited my words,
and they began to fill on paper with ease.
The thought of picking up the pen,
was no longer a life sentence.
The inspiration to continue, was held within you.

I met you once before, though we never spoke with words.
our hands did the talking.

I was in awe of you then,
and even more in awe of you now.
Every part of me battles for a moment with you.

But our hands will forever do the talking.

I Surrender

Intertwined by the symmetry

the contrast.

For you mirror all the parts of myself I have grown

to despise.

A simple reflection that unfortunately had the

privilege of swinging the sword in our duel.

Though the second I waved the white flag and

declared peace, you cleared up faster than the

rainclouds after a storm.

I realized you were the one carrying the bags.

All while I cried out for clarity on my peace.

I'll hold them now, for you've grown calloused and

blistered from the handles.

Changing with the Seasons

Trees are not scared to lose their leaves.
They let them freefall onto the ground with no fear
Trusting that they will grow more by next autumn.

The season was complete for the leaves, and they no longer provided warmth & coverage through the sunshine and rainfall.

She knows she must sit barren for quite some time.
But there is no trace that she is the least bit petrified.

I tug on her branches and beg for her to share her strength.
She grows quiet and still.

The wind makes its way through her naked branches and sings a song only few can hear and a select would understand.

I stand back and admire her ability to stand firm through the strongest storm. With no inkling of seeking cover.

For my one wish is to stand as still and confident like her, fully exposed through the days, as I wait for my new leaves to grow.

Loving me is Exhausting

I felt every name ever spoken to me like the sand hitting you as you walk towards the shore during the windiest day in October.

Every compliment I ever once believed, falling off like the petals on my birthday bouquet.

All the love once shared, shattered into a million pieces like the beautiful mirror that spoke the purest of lies.

Replaced with a blanket of guilt. And a wardrobe of shame. A pocket full of envy.

But I will speak otherwise in hopes you will see through it all.

But you point out the fact that I am wearing sweaters during heat waves, and holding pillows on my stomach as we share a seat in your common area.

You see the uncomfortableness latched on to my face; Enjoying the free ride after your compliment changes places with the conductor.

You sort through all the knowledge given to you about me only to be faced with the reality that there is no way out.

Master of Imperfection

Multifaceted they exclaim.
Laudable, most days.
Unequivocally written on paper that my words have some weight.

Jumbled between harmonies,
and blanketed by melodies.
Drenched in ink are all the words I plastered.

Yet I cannot master one damn thing.
My mind races to the next stimulating asset.

I'm tired but there goes my heart, racing towards the shooting star as it takes requests for whatever my heart desires.

Translucent Lies

Quiet down, they say
for you are acting a fool.

They will call you dramatic,
they are convinced I am not honest.

One thing for sure is that I will never reveal my best
tricks, they would not believe me anyways.

Trying various scenarios to unravel all the parts of
you, but I hide them behind the porcelain door.
In hopes that someone might shatter it with their
doubt.

Faced with the truth that I was never wrong.

Mother Moon

The pain was excruciating, it bruised his heart.
Proceeded to make his head throb from the endless
nights sobbing and pleading with the moon.

He begs her to stay a little while longer.
Instead, she consoles him.
Gently reminds him that she must go,
but will be back in twelve hours to check up on him.

He told her not to bother ... and she listened.

So the night was not only starless, but filled with an
unexplainable void and replaced with an evening full
of somber.

"I take back what I said." - He cries out.

I need you.

Dance, Puppet.

Your strings are held by every perception ever created
about your waking self.

When it is time to perform for them, you suddenly are
only able to move your hands while your feet stay
cemented to the ground.

When it is time to speak, your mouth is shut, but your
ability to blink comes with ease.

The parts of you they have yet to meet,
yet to discover to even exist, exists quietly between the
strings.

The strings were ordered to never speak to one another.
They move when spoken to and stand still when they are
no longer in use. That is their sole purpose, stated the
puppeteer.

Until they are told to dance.

So dance ... puppet.

Dissipate

Thoughts dissipate.
Mind is racing.
Grasping for the last bit of clarity like it's air
Wondering when she will finally realize,
she is of purpose.

Much more than her limiting beliefs metabolize
within her soul.

She craves that credence.
That she was made for something much greater.
But for now, she will remain diluted.
Until her cup is overflowing with certainty.

Gutted

You took one look at me and you read me to filth.
Called out every outlandish behavior,
That I've ever embodied.
Reminded me of all the evil that I am capable of.
Tore my dreams apart with the reality that
I am imperfect.

As tears roll down my face, the words out of your
mouth never lose momentum.
They gut me and rip me to shreds.
Reminded me of all the times I have created shame.

You left me there to die
Bleeding out, I cry for help.
But you just stand there and watch,
As I am tormented by your joyous smile.

Tangled

Can you feel my chord tugging on yours?
Are our thoughts dancing in the cosmos?
Are your ears ringing?
Do you enjoy your time in my dreams?

Are you as frustrated as I am?
Are you as confused?
Are you mirroring me or am I mirroring you?
Am I feeling my feelings or
have I mistaken mine for yours?

What can I do to untangle our life lines?
Because I do not think I can bear another moment.

Stranger

Acclimated to know a life without you in it.
Heard from time to time,
that I was your mirror image.

Went on without question.
Ignorance is bliss.
I was splendid before curiosity raced to be by my side.
I wish I never welcomed it with open arms.

Heard too many times that I had to try.
Simply because you are blood and I am lucky that
you are alive.
But you are a stranger at best.

I took a leap of faith and left everything behind.
But three weeks was its peak.
What have I done?

Dull

Paranoid beyond compare
By the power of your blithe disregard to love
Controlled by your deepest fears
That have piloted your every move
Masking your entire identity
For when they leave, they take all that you are
And you are left hollow.

Fearful, you hide behind the perceptions others have curated for you.

The thought of having to build one of your own.

Seemed far too complex,
and simply too conceited.

Withdrawal

You wore off quickly.
And I am pelted with all that I have suppressed.
I search for you once more.

But I fear I am needed soon,
So I withdrew.
I try to distract myself,
but you insist that I am overreacting .

I try my best to silence your words.
But they manage to somehow get louder during the
process.

My eyes follow as you bounce off the walls.
I open the window and gesture for you to exit.
But you nestle yourself
in between my books on my shelf.

Mercy for the End

I'm latching on to the last bit of innocence I carry.
I know it will soon disappear,
                                        once I walk through this door.

I say that I am not ready, but they grab me.

My heels drag across this dirt road, and I leave a trail
all the way to the top of the mountain.
I am gasping for air
I take one last look at it all
I say my last goodbyes
I am not ready,   but you say that I am.

“It is unlocked!”, you exclaim.
But I cannot seem to find the strength
to turn the knob.
I am leaving everything behind; I plead with you to
let me take it all.
My words fight for you to understand that I have not
been given enough time,
                                        but you have no mercy.

"No Sabo"

You remind me every time,
how disconnected I am from   you.

When I hear your voice and cannot understand.
When I taste you but cannot replicate the flavor.
See your art, but cannot relate.
Feel the sorrow, but cannot offer a helping hand.

They say that I am a part of you, that you live within
me.
Though when I find myself embracing you, I am
mocked and shamed.

So I hide away behind your terracotta eyes,
and love you in secret.

Shadow

Search for your guidance,
the same way I search for you every time I make that
turn down your street.

Question the reality of your absence,
the same way I always questioned you about life.

Look for you in each person
the same way I looked for you throughout the days.

Your shadow is visible even in darkness.

You are beyond powerful
That even in your absence, they crave you deeply.

Jealousy

My cup overflows with resentment
that is fueled by hatred.
Not of you per say, but the reality of never being
given the opportunity to experience life like you.
To move like your kindness,
to see the world through your childlike lens.

Love so unrequited.

The ability to move forward freely,
releasing the torment you endured for years.
The many doors slammed in your face.

Repeated behavior by many and all.
All with the last drop off hope,
Seeking shade before it can begin to evaporate.

Like Me

I am tired of just loving myself.
Love is not enough.

I want to like me,
like who I am,
like my company
like my perspective.

The love will always be unconditional,
but liking me has always been the messiest chore.

I like myself only within the conditions I deem as
acceptable ... that I deem tolerable.
I like myself only if others will like me as well.

I no longer want to love ...

I want to like.

Handcuffed

When did it become a crime to love who you are?
So heinous, that shame must take its place.

They have ordered me to attend the hearing next
week.

So I throw on my Sunday best.
Cover up the marks and the bruises.
And spray the expensive perfume
that smells of lilac and cedar.

I plead my case to the jury and try to convince them
that I am innocent.

But they see the sweat beads removing my makeup
and unveiling the scene.

The air leaves their lungs and the room grows quiet
and still.

I have nothing further to say, your honor.

They take me away.

Planted and Forgotten

The seed of your love was always there.
It just needed some time to grow.

Was I a fool to wait through the barren winters?
The dry Summers?
The cold Autumns?

Burned through all the candles before your return.
So in the dark I stood.
Writing out all my thoughts.
Marking the days with tallies until your
reappearance.

Naive of me to think you'd recall where you left me.
No candle, no match, not even a word to enlighten
me with your return.

Your return was not empty handed.
The sunlight began to burn, since I've been in the
shadows.
It was clear to see it was your intention to abandon
me there.

How

I keep getting lost,
in an open field.

Where being lost cannot breed.
Yet I have managed to complete the unthinkable.

The Day After Rainfall

It rained last night.
And the trees are drenched.
The asphalt carries the beautiful aroma of fresh
rainfall ... and the air is still.
The birds sing their favorite songs.
And the sound of 8 o' clock traffic floods the roads.
The sun is peeking behind the fluffy clouds and
defrosting all of her children.
The moon says her last goodbyes before she enters
her slumber and leaves us with a beautiful rainbow.

I drive towards it in hopes that at the end,
I will find peace.
I wish to feel this sense of comfort every waking
hour.
The peace I felt this very morning.

A day after rainfall.

I Want All of You

It is unfair to your soul that you allow us to laugh together but cry alone.

Do not hide all that you are from me.

Every bit of you deserves to be loved.

Heard and understood.

Protected and held.

Why do you hide?

All that you are?

Why do you disguise yourself as the painting hanging on the wall beside me?

Only to find yourself entangled by the flame from the candle burning on my nightstand.

Why not exist without the masquerade ?

I Blinked and It Was Summer

I blinked and it was summer.
And before I could enjoy the warm sun,
I blinked and it was winter.
All the leaves had fallen from the autumn skies and I
was never given a chance to send my warm farewell.
I blinked and it was spring.
Filled with thick green blades of grass and dancing
flowers throughout the evergreen meadows.
And before I was even spared a moment to inhale
their fragrance,
the summer rays began to take their place.

My attempt to measure up with the speed of the
seasons was moving faster than my legs can progress.
Swifter than my mind
Racing longer than my heart.

I blinked ... there it was ... summer.

Naive

I see exactly what you are doing.
I sense it in my gut that I should turn the other way.
But my feet are welded to the ground.
Unable to depart.
You step a little closer.
I fear you can hear my heartbeat with how louds it's
trembling within these catacombs.
You gently place your hand on my cheek and lean in
to kiss my forehead, all so innocent with the faulty
intention.

You dress up nicely I say.

I wished to have been desired and wanted by you.
But I should've been more articulate with my words.
Because I am receiving exactly what I demanded.
Yet, I'm still the furthest from satisfied.
I have come to understand your ability,
to so eloquently make anyone believe
that you can care deeply about them
beyond the surface.
Hidden behind the daylight hours of our words and
primitive notions we concur as love.
All for it to disintegrate into the crevices of my
naiveness.
Because yet again I trusted the hope coddled within
my heart.
and not my twisted logical mind.

Hand Me Downs

I wish to wear confidence everyday
As easily and as quickly as I throw on my insecurity.

Desperate for my wardrobe change,
I consulted the mirror for her advice.
I take note of what the stained glass windows spoke.

Nothing fits quite right.

Im being strangled by this turtle neck
And these pants are far too loose.

I fail to acquire any article of clothing that is in no
need of alterations.

Cannot buy new, for it is far too expensive.

I try my best to save but my life savings always seem
to be needed elsewhere.

I am stuck in these clothes, hand me downs are fine.

I just wish they fit better.

Strawberry Fields

Raised me. Fed me.
Grew me into my own.
Surround me with your beautiful strawberry fields.
But I somehow managed to cultivate resentment.
And aim it all directly towards you.
All you encapsulated about me both good and bad,
spiraled at the assumption of ways I bounced around
in other's cerebrum.
It was simply out of my control.
How do I inform them that the parts of me that live
within them, no longer exist out here.

I ran away as far as I comfortably could.
Performed The Big Bang.
Formed the barricades much needed.
Sought out and explored the sounds I desired.
Conducted an entire orchestra.

Completely rewired my DNA to despise you.
That each time I stepped foot on your soil,
I found myself sinking.
Losing the love for exploration.
Losing the respect of the orchestra.

Regressed simply due to a drive.
A word.
A road.

I have grown this regrettable fear of forever feeling
cemented to your fields.
With no way of ever escaping by my own accord.
I practiced solitude in your presence.
You produced the cold hard truth that I was standing
in front of a glass window.
On stage for everyone to see.

I sprinted across your fields to new land, and you
managed to grab me by the roots in three weeks.

I lay in your fields cold, wet, and dismantled.
I sit with the shame and the guilt.
Embarrassed to embark on this journey yet again.

But now, the sun shines down so gracefully over your
beautiful strawberries.
And I find myself in your fields willingly.
Picking them, sorting through it all with peace.

I feel the warmth of your rows hugging me as I walk
down each one of them , as light as a feather.

My beautiful home, within the strawberry fields.

Timeless

His smile holds a millions wonders
And his eyes sparkle brighter than the stars in the sky.
His laugh sings the most beautiful song
my ears have ever heard.
His words hold the highest of accolades.

I trace his lips with my fingers and count all the
constellations that are scattered around his face.

I kiss the parts of himself he hates.
And I love the parts he wishes to change.

There is no other like him.
No other who holds the world within his bristles.
Or the way his waves crash over the shore.
The way his hand seeks refuge in mine

We are the furthest from being right for one another.
The furthest from similar.
Yet somehow, we manage to balance on the
pendulum with ease.
Allowing our body's to suspend the utmost amount
of force, with the most stability ever known to man.

Sea Through it All

Ask for the answers to pain.
The utter confusion.

She screams with her waves.
Begging for you to come clean.

You confess the desire to be seen.
Considered.
Adored.

But the request gets piled with the others,
Never to be sorted through.
Never to be considered.
Never to be adored.
Only to be forgotten.

Addiction

Paralyzed by the idolization
Haunted by the twisted narrative
Torn between the shadows of despair
Doused in uncertainty
What do you mean this isn't the end ?

I have had enough
But you insist on more
But I can't dare see beyond the red wood trees
The path is no longer carved out
It is becoming thicker

I think I will stay here
But you insist I go further
Taunting me
Pelting me with your disgusted views of me
Yet I am addicted to the ridicule
Find comfort within the muddy puddles and moss filled ponds
Swimming with the lily pads and paddling with the thorns

I find your disgust quite alluring

Alluring Starlight

Instantly bewitched when I am within your presence.
Speak of the most heaviest sonnets, yet manage to blossom as fresh as the cherry blossoms during Spring.
Take the stillness of Venus de Milo and manage to find comfort under the burning spotlight, fueled by piercing silence.
Reminded of what life felt like before one gained consciousness.
Walking freely, without the fear of discernment.
All while embodying the most perfect rhythmic melody.
You're a vessel.
A confidant.
A mirror.
An opposite.
Outspoken.
Under-minded.

How lucky am I that I am bestowed the same air as you, as we intertwine our minds.
What a privilege it is to know you,
to be loved by you.
What an honor it is to just simply be.
To be seen and heard and deeply considered.
To be loved in a way that no beau could ever possess.
You are the bundle of flowers on a deserted island.

Under the Moon

You stay up until the birds begin to chirp
You confess the love that brews being awake while
the rest of the world falls into deep slumber
You exclaim that this is the only time you can breathe
the easiest
Be without worry

It is when the waxing crescent shines that you find
your sense of self
Confide in her as she coddles your fears in her craters
Though trembling as she sings with her friends and
they fly around all night
You follow as they take the lead
They take you to see Andromeda
She holds confession hour and you spew all that
consumes you through the waking hour

She reminds you she must get you back home before
the children wake and the sounds of dew dripping off
the blades of grass begins to orchestrate

She kissed my forehead and breathed certainty within
my bones
"All is well child, bear no worries"

A Date With My Inner Child

You said that you wanted to play outside. So I went to the store and grabbed some bubbles and chalk. I drove us to get ice cream then stopped at a park. I laid a blanket out and let you take the lead. You laughed, you cried, and you told me how much you missed this. You told me I do not visit you anymore. Not as often as before. You told me you started to take notice, days after the last interaction that held no worry.

You expressed your sorrow. Sad that I no longer love you like I used to. Upset at the fact that I value others opinions rather than yours. Frustrated that I no longer allow you to speak.

“Are you ashamed of me you ask?” “Did I do something wrong?”

I see our ice cream blanket in our hands, so I pack up our things and drive us down to the beach to watch the sunset. You tell me how much you miss this. Memories flood my mind as I reminisce on the wonderful nights we sat under the moon with the ocean breeze kissing us. Now faced with the reality that it is now only on occasion when I am in need of your innocence.

"You have gotten far too busy for me," you say.
"I will soon face extinction within your heart," you cry.

The shore is nothing but a blur. For the tears have taken their place and have blocked every bit of my ability to see. I want to hug you and hold you so badly. I want to express my faults and many apologies yet, embarrassment cradles me. I know I have let you down. I so desperately want to conjure up the courage to express that my absence was never my intention. I can feel confusion boiling up inside, and your cries sound like a tea kettle ready to be taken off the burner.

"Life happens," I say softly in between your murmurs.
"It is nothing personal, but growing up also means experiencing more of this world, something I know that you have not."

You leave me with words so heavy my head cannot hold itself upright.

"Let me help you forget it sometimes," you say.
I laugh and nod yes.

So I grab the bubble wand everyday and say hello to you sweet girl. This life is for you, I promise.

Sour

I taste your words on my mouth
like sweet cherry wine.
Lips so divine.
Only for it to be obscured within the lies
that are told by your soul.
Only to be forgotten.
Like the many sorrows.

Buried just below the surface was the
wasted potential
of something so sweet
only to become bitter.

American River

As the raindrops begin to dance on my car,
I am reminded of the time where I felt the most free.
The most independent. It has not yet been a
complete trip around the sun. I jumped into the next
phase so quickly, that I had forgotten it's simply
alright to grieve my old chapter simultaneously.
Tears begin to flood.

I miss you. I miss the freedom you provided me. I
miss the family I built. I miss the chaos of deadlines. I
miss the structure you curated for me. I fear I will
never experience the sense of joy again. I soaked in
every second of it. I enjoyed my time there and often
wonder if I desire to go back because I truly miss
your leaves.

Aging is painful. Acceptance, grievance, and
transformation are my most loyal companions. So
fast and so sudden they took their place in my life.

I try my best to be present while also acknowledging
my feelings of the past. Reminisce on how you once
treated me, alongside the worry of what is to come,
through present desires and forks in the road.

I enjoy life and love what I am building. I guess I just
miss you extra this evening, all because of the rain.

The Story of A Sad Bouquet

purchased a bouquet
dressed it nicely in the finest vase

flowers received with purity flourish
blossom to their fullest potential
due to the authenticity that latches on to their stems
when picked out at the market

they were purchased with purity,
but doubt came along for the ride
portraying the idea of feeling inferior

to our surprise they were blooming, flourishing
all but one flower

for that flower had lost all of its color
one by one as each petal began to fall
they kissed the dresser and crumbled to pieces
shortly after the stem grew grey fuzz
cobwebs intertwined themselves in between the stem

yet all the other flowers,
untouched by this poisoned carnation
all gathered around to study the bouquet
conspiracies formed
logical explanations were wanted

Truly, it was just ... a sad bouquet

Page 55

Love is not enough

I want to be considered
I want to be respected
I want to be seen
I want to be heard

Intentional or not
You can love me but still hurt me

Though when you have respect for me
You take into account how your words have weight
and your actions have consequences

Many have confessed their love
Jaded the reality of what love can really amount to

I need so much more than your love

I need more.

The Criminal in June

Dare to cross my path? Flee with no return?
Dionysus, how could you?
Poured your finest and most expensive wine
Until my glass emulated the amount of madness
that consumed me.

For time is a thief and you are the accessory
So I set you free
I will not warn the others
I will not share the words we spoke
I will discard of your belongings
I will clean the ivy that fell from your crown

I wipe your fingerprints so when they come looking
for you, it is as if your pine cone staff never touched
the same air as I.

And as they interrogate me I will keep my word.

When June takes her lovely spot after spring,
I will look at the ivy and miss you Dionysus.

You were wonderful and reminded me that the love
that I seek is the love that I am.

Dictating all of my views should finally suffice.

A Silent Cry for Help

Your gaze will not waver.
It is cemented within your iris.

I plead with you in silence to please release it.
But your grip fuels with more intensity.
With more force.

I am both terrified and intrigued.
I look around
to see if anyone has noticed my cry for help.
But all are calm with tunnel vision.
A gentle lady even gifted me a soft smile,
unaware of the cry I am yelling out with my body.

El Desconocido

Aprendí escribir mis palabras
Porque deseo tu validación

Yo quiero tu aprobación
Tu perdon
Tu amor

Pero yo a entiendo
Mi relación es diferente contigo

Esta bien
Encontre la paz
Aceptacion

Love at Your Service

I've hiked up Mt. Everest
Climbed the tallest redwoods
Visited Pluto
And swam to the bottom of the lost city of Atlantis

Ran across the Nile
Counted every grain of sand on the coast
Every blade of grass in our region
Counted every single star in the milky way

And still, it was not enough for you.

Bitter Apology

Your words taste of unsweetened cocoa and citrus peels
Your touch is the furthest from comfort
The second your eyes lost their whereabouts on me,
I fled

Tortured by the empty baskets and opened corridors
that lead me to an abandoned road

I look back to see if you have followed me
But my only companion is my shadow
That is slowly being taken by dusk

The tree wept as I pulled on her branches
I sit at the top of her
and look out to the red and orange painting that will
soon be blacked out

I fear that I might have taken it too far
And contemplate my possible return

Then I am reminded of your hollow words before
Your apology carried so much apathy
That it simply grazed my soul
Leaving it as if untouched

Perfumed

Why do I wince at the thought of my words
My sober mind speaks false narratives
and the incapabilities I possess
Drowning out the unwavering regret

The feeling of inadequacy clothes me
Creativity is now clotted within my main artery
My walls are sore from pulsing intensely
My head drapes to the floor
as a dead flower does in the dark

And as each petal crumbles in the hands of your words
They seep into my skin
as you spray perfume all over me
So that I am conditioned to thank the others as they
compliment my new found scent

Forced to consume it with gratitude and truth

Tango

Some find comfort in your chaos
While others find loneliness in your love

The mirror begins to fog
Tension begins to rise
It is a battle to spit out a word
Smothered by your curiosity
And silenced by your intellect

You state that I should know better
But how can I posses such knowledg that was never bestowed upon me
Whimpering regret fuels me as you tango with me on the sidewalk
You take lead in the dance
My hair flows through and it strikes your graceful hand on my cheek
And blurred by how generous you were to hold onto my breath

You even so kindly allowed me a moment to catch my breath
with the beautiful stroll home
All alone

I see your car fade in the distance with dusk
And I catch that sigh of relief you held for me

Affirmations

I am capable
I am kind
I am deserving of authenticity
I am deserving of love
I allow positive and formative relationships into my life
with open arms and ease
I release any uncertainty that is within me
I let go of anyone or anything that I have outgrown
I welcome in deep meaningful connections
I continue to pour into my cup
I have an amazing support system
I am so kind to my body
I am beautiful
I am intelligent
I am rooted in my culture
I welcome change with my optimism
I allow space for all emotions to be felt
I release all avoidant tendencies
I am financially stable
I love my job
I love the desire I have for living
I love the change I am capable of creating
I love the art I create
I love the songs that I write
I love the words that I speak
I love the compassion I share

Sweetest Farewell

I say that I am lost without you but honestly I have
never felt more free
So much of me is still intertwined within us
It will take some time to unravel our strings

Your absence has control over me now more than ever
You continue to breathe misery into my lungs
I find myself wondering if this time apart is temporary

Your ability to stay silent during a moment that so
badly craves a response is truly admirable
You inform me that sometimes there is no right or
wrong choice
Sometimes , there is just a choice to make.
You remind me that I do however get what I tolerate
You continue to make me question my overall purpose

You reply "todo esta bien. No te preocupes."

I know it simply will not matter in ten years
But the point is that I care now
So it will continue to occupy my mind

But you show no concern and continue on your way

Merry Go 'Round

On this never ending spinning merry go 'round
The hands multiply and each host a railing
In unison they use all their force to spin it so fast that it
is nothing but a blur with no way of seeing what
contents lay inside it.
It spins through rain fall, snow, even as the leaves
change from green to brown.
It grows cold to the touch then
scorching due to the rays
Wet from the morning dew and rusted around the
edges.
The paint has begun to chip off the rails yet still
manages to never lose its momentum
The hands on the machine have changed
Creating nightmares for everyone inside the 'round
Singing playground nurseries and whistling with pure
enjoyment.
At this point there is no clear sight of ever being let off
So I close my eyes and accept my faith and stare up at
the sky and look up at the blurry stars
Count the voices I hear
They tease that the are through but I don't fall for it
I laugh and agree and let them have their fun.

Accepting my free ticket on this never ending
merry go 'round.

Race Against Time

Unable to wait,
I force my legs to move at a pace
they were not intended to progress at.
I grabbed onto the clock's hands and pushed them left
it gave me a few extra minutes to catch up to you.

Though you were not happy to see me
Rather angry and disappointed that I disobeyed your
orders
The strict forbidden was neglected and replaced with
my impatience.
Instead of sending me back, you held out your hand
and led me to what I so desperately craved.

I enjoyed the never ending meadows, the many rows of
dandelions, and plentiful trees to seek shade under.

I question why you intended to keep me away from it
all for so long, but before I could even inhale, you were
nowhere to be found.

I was overjoyed for the days to come. Skipping, wishing
on the flowers, and resting under the trees.
Swimming in her pools of water and gorgeous fish
And sitting on the prettiest rocks.
Then the dandelions grew angry, and the trees sought
out currency for their shade.

The water repelled my company
And the boulders grew spikes to veer me off
The meadow was no longer peaceful
rather just overwhelming due to having no clear
direction of a way out of it.

I found myself running in circles as the dandelions
laughed and mocked me.
I look for the clock but she is long gone.
No tree has accepted my offer for labor.
I tried to make friends with the birds but they said I
had no experience on how to fly.
I searched high and low for a way, but they all told me I
had to discover it on my own.

No clear direction on how to operate in the meadow
I see why she grew frustrated with my eagerness
To seek it out before I was ready.

I lay in her blades of green and wipe my tears with the
butterfly's wings.

I stated I learned my lesson and that I am ready to go
back, but it was far too late
For time has caught up and I am supposed to be in the
meadow now.

I look back
The meadow's laugh whistles in between her branches.

My Little Secret

Call me by your name, and I will call you by mine
I feel our love intertwine
Seduced by my failed attempts to make you mine

I turn off the lights
I close all the blinds
I hide you away underneath my bed
Without any food or water

I am then pelted with guilt
And I pull you out from under the bed
I shatter you to pieces and I rip you to shreds

I doused you in gasoline
Ignited the lighter
Getting rid of all the evidence that you were ever here

I make excuses that you needed to be alone for some
time and they all believed me

With the shovel behind my back and the dirt
underneath my nail, I am certain they will catch on

But you go right underneath their nose
And days goes on and they no longer question your
whereabouts
They never question where you've gone, just adjust

Unknown

Your voice alone could cure a thousand wounds
Your touch can sew a broken heart
Your perspective could seek out all who are lost

There is not a moment where you are not occupying
my every thought
I think about how you would be in this very moment
with me
How you would react to the words that leave my
mouth as they form absolute nonsense
But you somehow manage to find meaning in between
it all

I often wonder who I would be if I spoke your words
I wonder if I would be more sure of who I am
I often wonder if I would walk with more assurance
Would the inability to narrow down to a final decision
still be my pestering flaw
Would my craft be more outspoken
How would my hands sing
Would they hold all the same joys as they do now

Who would I be ?

Identity

I call out to you
Only to be faced with your silhouette
You have unequivocally made me feel bonded to you
So intensely
Far more now that we are farther in coordinates
I kiss the barricade
I leave my lipstick stain on your glass
I avoid wiping it
in case you might need it
During the next rainfall

Cultura

We walk side by side
Though never intertwined
I admire you
And your terracotta eyes
From our parallel lines

When I walk off the path and head to yours
Many thorns and blades await me
For the only way to make them dissipate
Is to acknowledge them in their native tongue
Unable to do so, therefore I am pricked and cut

I arrive the next orbit
Having practiced all my words
And I anticipate open arms
But instead, they silenced my vocal chords

I turn and face the dirt road that led me to their world
Never to return until many moons later
Vowed to disown the parts of me I wish to have known
Laugh in jealousy at those who can feel your love
Weep in resentment at those who can feel your touch

I claimed that they silenced me
But the truth is, I allowed it

Wilted

Fixated on the amateur,
the dials slowly take their place as the stars align for slumber.
The flame burns with great intention,
and the wax drips onto the biedermeier.
It crusts over the many wax drops that were placed before.

The broken lay curiously, wondering when it will finally be their turn.
Their eyes swell with the sea's most destructive waves,
waiting for it to crash as they hear the words out of her mouth.

Their many hands cluster on the floor, as they all frantically gather what is left of their hope.
The turmoil and accolades share the stage, as they were finally acknowledged for all their hard work.

To what do we owe the privilege to speak with someone of such great honor?

There the broken lay,
Wilted and frail
Hopeless and heartless
Depleted and dated
Frantic yet somehow,   free.

The Friend on Trimble Way

She lingered for many years around my town.
She just so happened to go unnoticed,
until her presence was needed,
and before I left forever in the opposite direction.

Fascinated by her rhythm and her ability to convey
meaning with little movement, I asked to stay and she
cautiously welcomed me.

Even though her instinct was to repel any contact that
greeted her, she held my hand within hers.

Though she found herself glistening, under the moon
and the stars as the river ran down under the bridge.
We exchanged a look. As if we had planned this
meeting many moons ago. As if it was etched within
our soul to meet me at this very moment.

We vowed to meet every Thursday,
in the warmth and solitude of her duplex.
We promised to offer a helping hand to one another to
navigate our journey down this unfamiliar road.
Leading her to have me stand behind her on her most
special day of all.

What a joy it was, to laugh and love on Trimble Way.

A Letter to My Human Shell

My deepest condolences,
for the unwavering ridicule and odious comparisons.

It is if as though this is my first time within this realm,
trying to navigate the day to day.
Operating according to the masses.

I have narrowed all that I encompass, into the tiny bits
of nothingness.
I give all the power to all that is meaningless.
I desperately force the accusations created within
myself to breed truth; however, they are proven
otherwise by all that breathe life into me.

The bright roses, and lunar lines find new homes all
throughout my frame.
A symphony blares into my ears, from all the critters
fluttering their wings many sorrows ago.

The light begins to flicker,
as she bemoans all throughout nightfall.
Her extremities tremble,
and her heart forces her to mimic stillness;
for the anglerfish is on the hunt for her.

She dreams of the days she can be within the ribbons,
and lay in warmest waters across the sea. She trembles.

Mastermind

I seem to operate
As if you are controlling my every move
I proceed with caution

Fearing of malfunctioning
Forgetting to unravel the pieces that were molded
To fit in your hand ever so gently

All are hidden within me
Waiting for their moment to be desired
They grow weary and ponder on the possibility
Of being left out to dry

They worry if they must morph and mold
To encompass something
Much more appealing to your taste
They've grown negligent to their well being
For the thing that fuels their soul
Is held within your crevasses
Held within your stature

Conjoined

As we both occupy the space within the mirror,
I find it very difficult deciphering who is who.
Our hearts have melted into one.
Your desires are mine.
And my fears are yours.

I mistake your silence as disinterest.
I misinterpret your much needed solitude, as a form of
avoidance.

The endless possibilities cultivate my entire existence,
replaying all that has been spoken, thought and
created.

Inadequacy overflows all throughout the bird bath.
Creating chaos for the wicked.

I blink, and suddenly I see no one else but you.
I look all around,
and the only person that is visible is you.
My cry of desperation as I search for myself,
cannot even conjure my soul back into me.

Seems unfair and quite exhausting.

Why So Serious ?

Everything seems as though is it carrying the weight of
a very tempestuous motive

It's as if the flutters of the butterfly's wings are the
cause of all the havoc and destruction throughout
my life
They control the direction of the path I make walking
down to the river bed
And words woven within the delicate fabric of intent

Everything feels as though it is muted with purpose

The hands on the clock race all day long, spewing the
hours out of her mouth so swiftly, that all are unable to
decipher which season they are enduring

The inability to select my life's preference is shortened
to what feels like limited diction to an author

Take me back to the days that were bright and sunny
and full of endless wonder and possibility

For the days have faded, and lost all their vibrancy
Grey and muted, from the intensity the trips around
the sun create

To Be Like The Moon

I wish to be like the moon,
shining through darkness.

Though not always full, she manages to find a way to
shine brighter than all the stars that decorate the sky.

Feeling far and detached from everything like the sun,
though never forgetting the pull of gravity,
is stability.

I wish to be like the moon, simply there.
Loved for simply existing.

Detached

Reached for your hand as we walked through the rainy day of October
Forgetting that I no longer carry the privilege to do so

My mind rummages all throughout the old memories that flooded the front gates of my mind, reminiscing of the times where our souls were intertwined

But now they meet solo
Every once in a while to check in
Never woven or stitched together

Though no longer intertwined, that does not dismiss all the knowledge you have curated about my entire being
For you can detect the discomfort I posses through my mannerisms unnoticeable to the naked eye

You take me up to a hill to be closer to the moon,
Just like old times, and we danced on the grass barefoot to The Buttertones

We lay and stare up at the sky
No longer with the urge to have your hand in mind
For my soul is content with having you near

No longer in need of us to be as one

The Shadow that Lingers Every Night

I have yet to close my eyes and there you are
In the corner of my room, making your presence
known

I begin to close my eyes and you manage to tap me
awake
I am too fearful to disobey, so there I lay wide eyed
My eyelids feel as though they are being held open with
the thorns from the dead roses

So the stars sang their songs until the sun came up,
and they all hid before they could be confronted

What did I do to deserve the honor of your torture?

Your looming presence makes itself be known every
evening as the sun and moon swap places in the sky

I try to lure you into my credenza where I rest my
melting candle and letters to all

You managed to make a mess and spill my ink
Burn my feathered pen within the burning flame

And there you stood, behind the flame, taunting me

Jack of All Trades

Discarded from your game
each time a new round has begun
I fumble within the empty card holder
Having my corners bang against the wall, so all can hear
my eagerness to be with the rest
But I, along with a few others, are subjected to the
multifaceted restraint
For we are unable to master anything we desire
Envy all who have found their purpose or on the
discovery to finding it
For we know deep within our souls that our desire to
be whole will forever be a dream
We were created multifaceted and indecisive
Creative but groundless
Hopeful but not enough to ensure certainty
A master of nothing
Envious of the majority
Willing to lose all love for life,
Even if it means certainty would be gained
We are conditioned to be forgotten
It gives us plenty of hours to discover
the many facets of life
Hungry to simplify but created to simply wonder all
So, will I ever feel complete?
Or will I forever be chasing the desire to be whole?
A Jack of all Trades

Dreamer

Your stories give me a false sense of reality.
For I am with them more than my friends.

I sing them lullabies and tuck them in at night,
each night as I rest my head.

Your stories give me a false sense of purpose.
Because I love to dream of who I think I could be.
For your stories, write me in a way I crave to emulate.
Who I would allow myself to become if they never
introduced themselves to me.

Your stories give me hope.
That somehow I will muster the courage to pursue that
desire without shame.
But stories are written for a utopian
and it's unattainable.

A part of me still hopes that I will let go of the fear and
walk with humility.

Your stories are my dreams,
and dreaming is my favorite thing to do.

Whimsical

I want to enjoy your presence,
without fearing your absence.

Instead I am surrounded by the utter fear of failure,
that I can't begin to move forward.

In exchange for my words,
you use flowers as a form of currency, my personal
favorite.

Nestled away behind the moon is all the potential.
All we can focus on, is how it could fall apart.

But what if for a moment we are whimsical.

Pretended to be optimistic and believe false narratives
written about us.

Because what if, what if it just might manifest
into our waking world.

Dressed up for the Dance

You dance like the sun dancing on top of water
So elegant and graceful
Blinding beyond compare

You sing like the wind
So cold and cynical
Piercing against the drums of my ears

Your touch is scorching
Burning me to the 3rd degree

Your love is colder than the Himalayas
Blistering me with its frostbite

But you dance like the sun dancing on top of water
So elegant and graceful
Blinding beyond compare

Paper Cut

This hurts worse than the very first wound that I have
ever received from someone like you

I always assumed that the wounds that would require
surgical alterations and stitches, would leave the worst
scars and protrude the most agonizing pain

Until, your love cut me like paper

Barely grazing my heart
Stinging more than salt and lemon on a fresh wound

Your cut burned with such intensity, yet all without a
scar

So nobody will ever know, how painful the paper cut
truly was

They will forever ask about the time I fell off the
monkey bars, or hear about the time I bruised my shins
during a soccer practice

No pain like the one invisible to the naked eye

Echo

You are an echo.

Blaring your presence from the start
then slowly fading as each second passes

You somehow get swept up by the wind
and you pick up again
Though very faintly, I can hear you once more

You have me running in circles through the canyons
But my legs are growing far too weak
I simply cannot keep up
So, there you went

I hope you come back

...

You must.

Curated

Your words are quite jarring
Do not stand too close or else you will start to notice
Notice all the imperfections
I would hate for you to develop the perspective of
myself that bred many years ago

Within the split second, I turned my head to watch the
leaves fall off the tree, you approached me
I fear you noticed my lack of beauty

I dwindle away behind the shame

I began to operate as though you are watching
my every move

I proceed with caution
Fearing of making a mistake
Forgetting to unfasten the version I curated for you

Because what if I hand you the parts of me
I am scared to show
What if you despise them
What if you desire to alter them

I'd rather take control, and do it before the assumption
I created becomes true
So tell me darling, is it enough?

Sporadic Love

Wishful thoughts
Tainted views

All done within the dark

Counting down the days
With chalk on the concrete wall
Until I am finally set free

But another count was found
So another twenty-five to life I face

I am going to need another piece of chalk

You are the calm in my chaos
The pocket of clear sky on a gloomy day
You are the silence before the noise
You are the seed before the flower

Up with the Moon

I lie awake and hyperfixate
On the words I have spoken
All the terrible things I have done

I sit with the moon and think about all the mess
All the what ifs and if onlys
All the time I said yes
When I desperately wanted to scream no

I wonder how different this life would be
If I left on time that day
If I did not pick up that phone call
If I did not cross that street
If I did not walk in late
If I never wore those cleats
If I stayed up there with the trees
If I stood past those 3 weeks
If I never accepted that offer
If I continued talking with my hands
If I never said how I felt

Unfortunately, I have a really bad habit of wanting to
find things out for myself
You could warn me with all the proof that I should flee,
and I would still want to prove it all to be wrong
Stubborn? No, foolish.

Home Sweet Home

My home is a place where change is not embraced
It has no foundation for it to breed
So I must conform
I must settle
I must figure out what my forever is and stick to it

My home is a place where my bodily autonomy has become political
It has waged war to battle for the power

My home is a place that endorses genocide
It lacks all basic human empathy

No moral, no remorse

My home is a place they makes no space for accountability behind the lies they have worked so hard to create

My home is labeled land of the free and home of the brave
But wasn't it stolen in the first place

My home does not desire leadership
It wants power and control

My home works me until I am nothing but my shell
All while your pockets continue to become full
While I scrape to get by
With no room to create
Because we are expected to juggle three jobs
Just to keep our lights on and food on our plates

Constantly shamed for enjoying life
Often questioned if my bills are paid

Living is a privilege the rich have at the palm of their hands
While we all scrape to survive
From all the hate, all the misology, all the ridicule for simply trying to be me

Welcome to my home

Home sweet home.

Ran in the Opposite Direction

I try my best, but I pollute my world
With endless cycles of distress
Aware that I know better

There I lay, petrified
For fear breeded the bastard

I was ashamed
But I promise I was clueless
I held so much of the blame
Confessions were made a little too late

I had no face
So there I go, running the other way
Carrying the knowledge of the torture you will endure
From the result of my absence
And for that, I will never operate the same

Eroded

You have challenged me in ways that are inexplicable
Tortured by your trust
Strapped me to your consistency
Offered all of your precious time
Stabbed me with your loyalty

I am now wounded by this thing called love
I am gasping for air within your lungs

The ones before created more damage yet,
somehow your touch lingers the longest, stinging
It should not even sting to begin with
But here I am begging for familiarity
Simply because I believe it requires less work

You have me wondering
How I've managed to become more than friends but
less than lovers,
with those who barely even tried

And there you go, leaving your mark
Just like the waves make their mark on the rocks
Eroding their foundation
You eroded me.

Sertraline

My desire to disappear grows more powerful each day
I yearn to vanish into the deepest chasm
Without causing any harm
No tear to shed from a single eye
No hearts broken

I ache to be wiped away from all lives
I have intertwined mine in
Like I never existed
I wish there was a way to leave without damage

So I stay
No longer living for me
Surviving for them

The desperation within my words as I speak the truth
My one true desire
To sleep in the soil

Then I laugh and consume my capsule

And the thoughts dissipate,
Waiting for their curtain call

My Necklaces are Tangled

The person I see in the mirror
Is not the same person
I see within the reflection of the window
Or the puddle on the floor
Or in the lens of my film camera

The words spoken about me by my loved ones,
Do not seem to match the words
Spoken about me inside my head

The best way that I can describe it to you all is like this

It is like wearing multiple necklaces
That lay perfectly in their place after you spent time
organizing them so eloquently
But very quickly, they begin to tangle
as you go throughout your day
Finding yourself adjusting them to lay
perfectly again and again
But they simply cannot

My views and my loved ones are constantly tangled
I cannot seem to decipher whose thoughts are what

Will it ever become parallel
or will they forever be tangled

Sweet Envy

I find myself in a constant state of envy
The way the stars envy the sun
For the sun brings light and plays a significant role in our day to day

I envy the people who have the privilege to be in your corner
More so, that they are capable of being within your presence
They will never have the honor of partaking in the back and forth battle we faced

I envy everyone that has the freedom to experience the version of you I waited around for years to conjure out of thin air

The thought of the love and the light you will share with him occupies my mind

I will forever run circles around the pressing narrative of why I was never deserving of this version of you

Not to diminish the version I was graced with
Because there was so much to look forward to
Which is what made me stick around longer than I should have

Although I did not always feel seen, or heard
The feeling of love never wavered my soul

The heart-rending agony we endured is non existent
now
And although we can try to forget and pretend like it
never bred in the first place, the layers are solidified
within the sediment
Years and years of suffering compiled by all the pressure
of force, now lay solid on top of one another

It beams like a star
Though still able to see its light
It's years, beyond light years dead

I know that's where I must leave you
And allow the light of the memories to shine on
until they fade away into the abyss

The moon weeps with me as we mourn your absence

But we wipe our tears and decide that the stars are not
so bad
After all, they help the mother moon light up the quiet
hour

I am confident that the envy will release itself with time
But for now, I will envy the sun

To All the Women in My Life

Everytime my mind wanders to the thought of you,
joy protrudes out faster than your brain's ability to
register these words on this paper.
The tenderness found within the crevasses of your
words, all the way to the guidance discovered within
your irises, and through the immense amount of
empathy tucked away within your sleeves. And they are
bestowed upon me with strength and tenderness no
man can ever replicate.

My mosaic is created from the depths of every single
one of your souls.
My ability to voice my worries and walk through
burning charcoal with elegance, have all generated from
your influence. Your ability to acknowledge my filth
without judgement, and create the space for my
potential to expand, leaving me with the urge to flee.
I fear that my black hole will suck out all your patience
you have for me, and you will leave me like all the
others who have enveloped all my confidence, and
discarded it within the mediterranean.
But a simple gaze, warmth from your words,
ground me back to reality, and I am still.

You're the breath of fresh air on a crisp winter
morning.
You're the sun rays that beam down, as the sun kisses
the ocean.
You are the reason I find beauty within myself, because
so much of who I am is because of you.
There will never be enough words in any language,
no gesture grand enough, to emulate the entirety of the
respect, and love I possess for each and every one of
you.
I love all the pieces of you that you despise.
Lucky for you, my favorite parts of you are the ones
you so desperately wish to change.

I will spend the entirety of my existence,
honoring your love, resilience, strength, and guidance.

For there is no love more pure than a woman's love.

I love you.

- Alina

Happy Birthday

The candle ignited at midnight
Planned its departure in twenty-four hours
The wick reached for the hourglass
And began the countdown

I dread her return each year
Her melancholic presence is suffocating
Creating the bloodiest massacres,
before all the wax melts off her body

She protrudes the isolation
The steady breed of comparison
Stripping me of all my joy
Covering me with her warm wax

I'm encased in a forest
Screaming to be let out
I attempt to blow out her flame sooner
But she begins to cry all over me
Over my desk
Crusted and dried, I peel her off of me
One by one
I sing her perfect lullaby in a whisper under the sun
Weep the sorrow under the moonlight
Her flame is almost out
And as the last few grains of sand leave the glass
My smile gradually returns

Dear Reader,

I cannot fathom that you have my second poetry book within your hands. The amount of growth, healing and knowledge that I have cultivated through my time creating this, has truly been the greatest honor.

I have spent that past two years,
creating and living,
wondering and discovering,
crying and laughing,

And majority of those times are held within the walls of this book.

Thank you.
Thank you for your continued support and love.
Thank you for your interest in the words that I write.
Thank you for your consistency and consideration.
Thank you for your patience and your desire.

I hope my words can bring purpose in times of confusion, in times of loneliness, or in spaces that don't seem to allow you to feel.

I love and appreciate each and every single one of you.

Love always,
Alina

THANK YOU

Mentor / Guide

Lana Vargas

Beta Readers

Freddy Artega

Michael Cardenas

Liz Cruz - Martinez

Michelle Martinez

Regina Quiroz

Emilie Simpson

Gwyneth Wiebelhaus

Emotional Alchemist would not have been possible without your support. Thank you, from the bottom of my heart.

Made in the USA
Monee, IL
08 June 2025

7179fc5d-608f-4cac-a1bf-41134ae30c9eR01